MARLBOROUGH & THE KENN

MARLBOROUGH & THE KENNET

Photography by Jonathan Gaunt
Text by Michael Pooley

ACKNOWLEDGEMENTS

I would like to thank the following people for their help, advice and kindness:
Mr & Mrs R. Atkinson, Bishops Cannings P.C.C., Mr. R. J. Butler, Mr P. Chapple-Hyam
(Swettenham Stud), Mr. V. Chinnery, Mr A. Cooper, Mr S. E. Cowdry, Mr P. de Savary,
Mr and Mrs D. Dickens, Duchess of Somerset's Hospital, Mr & Mrs K. Duddy,
Mr & Mrs M. Giddings, English Heritage, Mr C. Hibberd, Mr D. Hicks (Wroughton
History Group), Mr. D. Hill, Mr H. Hyams, The Rev. P. Hyson, Kennet & Avon Canal
Trust, Mr. H. Keswick, Lloyds of Great Bedwyn, Marlborough College, Merchants House
Trust, Lady Moyne, National Trust, Ms E. Perkins, Mr D. Redfern (Littlecote Leisure Ltd),
Dr G. F. Reitmaier, Mr & Mrs A. Robb, Mrs. J. Robertson, Miss J. Ross, Mr G. Stradling,
Wadworth Brewery (Devizes), Mr & Mrs Wally, Walter T. Ware Ltd.

Special thanks to Mrs C. Gaunt, Mr & Mrs T. Mabbutt

ISBN 0 95233800 9

First published in 1994 by
White Horse Bookshop Ltd
136 High Street, Marlborough, Wilts. SN8 lHN

Typesetting by Impact Images, Hoe Benham, Newbury, Berkshire

Printed in Singapore by Eurasia Press in association with
Hugh Stancliffe Associates P.O. Box 113, Marlborough, Wiltshire SN8 1RL

Captions to photographs on preceding pages
Half title page: Downland, Membury - Page 2 : Silbury Hill - Title page: Smiths of Marlborough - Opposite: The Kennet, Chilton Foliat

INTRODUCTION AND PHOTOGRAPHIC NOTES

THE KENNET
RAMSBURY

Throughout history this river has played a central role in the lives of everyone in the Kennet valley. Dozens of mills along its entire length were dependent upon it, stretches of the valley were farmed as water-meadows, and the purity of its chalk filtered water led to the development of trout farming and for a period this century the Kennet supported a substantial watercress industry in the Ramsbury area. Nowadays the Kennet is chiefly valued for its trout fishing and its role in providing a natural habitat for wildlife. A unique environment which must be preserved from the twin dangers of pollution and excessive abstraction.

This book is an attempt to show the variety and beauty of the Downs and villages surrounding Marlborough. The visitor to the area can enjoy busy market towns steeped in history, but within a short distance can see stunning downland scenery, forests, villages and historical sites.

Many limit their visit just to Marlborough and Avebury often missing many of the surrounding delights of the Wiltshire downland landscape. Throughout this book the photography and text takes you on a journey from Marlborough, west along the Bath road to Avebury and Devizes returning eastward through the beautiful Vale of Pewsey. The travellers return by Marlborough and the Savernake exploring to the north and east as far as Kintbury. The boundaries of this book can be reached by car within thirty minutes from Marlborough through quiet lanes and villages.

Although most people visit in spring and summer the beauty and peace of the area can be enjoyed throughout the year. The stark morning light in winter holds a beauty all of its own as does Savernake in autumn. For the lover of the English landscape a walk to Barbury, Liddington or Martinsell on a clear day must rival many a foreign destination.

The majority of locations in this book can be visited but often the photographs are taken on private land with the kind permission of the owners.

The entire book has been photographed using my trusted Hasselblad camera and a variety of lenses and filters. A sturdy tripod and a small pair of stepladders, plus a willing wife to carry them, proved to be invaluable. Kodak Kodachrome and Ektachrome film has been used throughout the book. All landscape photography is capturing a moment in time, often waiting long periods for that moment to happen, sometimes it does not, thus requiring several return visits. The photographs chosen for this book are often not always the best viewpoints due to roadsigns, wires, television aerials, parked cars and of course the budding film star you do not require in the composition.

HUGHENDEN YARD
MARLBOROUGH

Once owned by the Free family - prominent in Marlborough for many years - who originally came from Hughenden in Buckinghamshire as stonemasons to work the local sarsen stone. Now opened up with an adjoining yard to form a pleasant parade of small specialist shops and a restaurant.

ST. PETER'S CHURCH
MARLBOROUGH

The first view of Marlborough from the south west as one descends Granham Hill on the Pewsey road. To the left lies Marlborough College and to the right of St Peter's Church the beginning of the High Street. There is evidence of an earlier church on the site but the present fine building dates from 1460 and it was here that the future Cardinal and Chancellor, Thomas Wolsey, was ordained in 1498. This end of the High Street escaped the great fire of 1653 and consequently some of the oldest houses in Marlborough are found in the narrow street on the north side of the church.

MARLBOROUGH COLLEGE

Hunger, bullying, fighting and flogging characterized the early years of College life culminating in 1851 with open warfare between the boys and the authorities. Conditions have improved markedly since then - not least with the arrival of girl pupils in recent years. The College now enjoys a high reputation with an excellent academic record. John Betjeman's *Summoned by Bells* includes a good account of his life at the College in the 1920's. The College has pioneered the idea of a residential Summer School at the end of July and early August making use of its excellent facilities to offer a range of weekly courses for adults and children.

MARLBOROUGH COLLEGE

Built in the early years of the 18th century for the Duke of Somerset, this magnificent porticoed mansion became in 1751 the Castle Inn which in its heyday was one of the finest coaching inns on the Bath road. Forty coaches a day are said to have changed horses here. But the prosperity of the coaching era died swiftly with the coming of the railway to Swindon. In 1843 it was reopened as Marlborough College with 200 pupils and 6 masters.

MERCHANT'S HOUSE MARLBOROUGH

The Merchant's House at 132 High Street is one of the finest houses in Marlborough and has survived in a remarkably complete state, with much of its original interior decoration. It is being expertly restored to its former glory and will soon re-open as a Museum of 17th century town life. The Great Parlour has its original 1656 floor-to-ceiling oak panelling and impressive stone fireplace with decorative wooden overmantel. Part of the ground floor now houses the Museum shop and guided tours of the whole building can be arranged by appointment.

CHANDLER'S YARD MARLBOROUGH

One of a number of lanes leading off the High Street. The building on the right belonged to Chandler the saddler from 1820 to 1924 and hence its name. An earlier name was Horsepassage Yard and tradition has it that the Royalist cavalry in December 1642 forced its way into the town down this lane from the Common. The Town, unlike the Castle held by Lord Seymour, opposed the Royalist cause and paid dearly in property, if not life, with 53 houses being destroyed during the war.

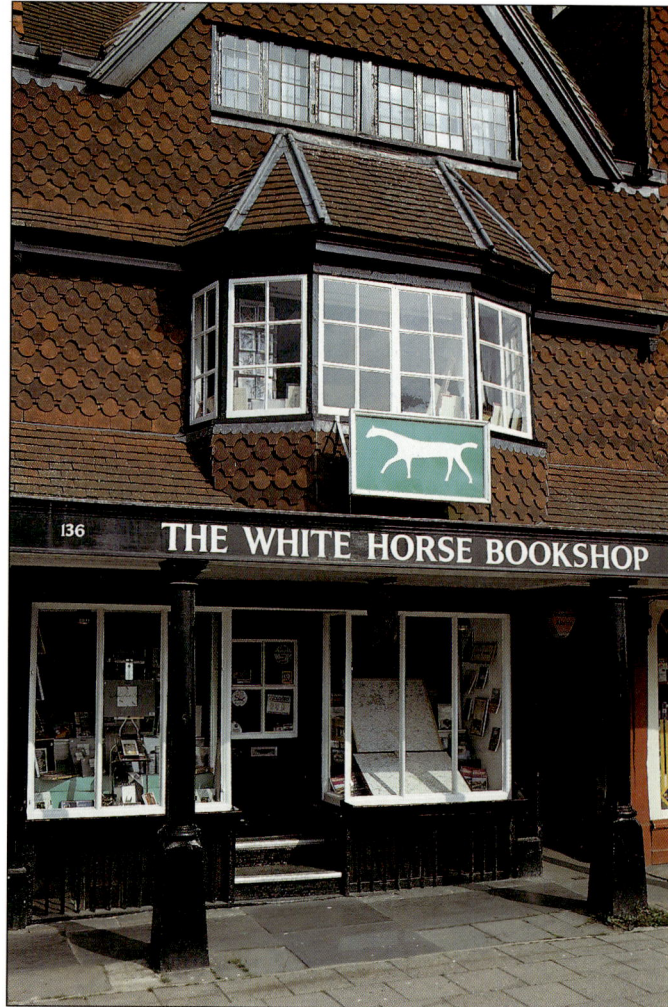

THE WHITE HORSE BOOKSHOP MARLBOROUGH

Recent restoration work has confirmed that much of the interior of this building predates the great fire, although the thatched roof and all the frontage were destroyed. A leaded window on the top floor visible in Chandler's Yard survived the fire. The shop was originally four separate dwellings. The oldest at the front and the back with a courtyard and well in between. This gap was infilled in the 18th century with two cottages.

ST. MARY'S CHURCH MARLBOROUGH

Overlooking the Green to the east and the long wide High Street to the west, St Mary's Church can be said to be at the heart of Marlborough. The fine west door is proof of its Norman origins but the church we see today was entirely rebuilt within the shell of the old following the disastrous fire of 1653. It is an impressive example of unadorned Puritan architecture. The cost of this restoration was met by a collection throughout the country ordered by Cromwell. An entry from the parish register of the little Somerset village of Isle Abbotts reads 'Collected in the Parish Church of Ile Abbotts and from house to house the summe of one pound twelve shillings and three pence towards the releife of the Towne of Marleborough which was consumed by fire in the space of three or foure houres ....'

THE KENNET MARLBOROUGH

The Kennet flowing through the College grounds towards the Pewsey road bridge. On the left side of the river there is a footpath passing Treacle Bolley, the site of an old mill, leading to Preshute Church. From this on the left on Granham Hill can be seen the White Horse cut in 1804 by the boys from the Marlborough Academy. This then occupied the Georgian building in the High Street which is now the Ivy House Hotel.

PRIORY GARDENS MARLBOROUGH

The original Carmelite Priory founded in 1316 and the hundred year older Gilbertine Priory in the Salisbury road have long since been demolished. The present building dates from 1820 and was for some years used by the College as one of its boarding houses. The lovely gardens which run down to the Kennet are open to the public.

POLLY TEAROOMS
MARLBOROUGH

Few visitors can resist the charm of the Polly and rightly so. But they should consider themselves fortunate that the ground floor of this early Georgian building survived the recent fire which destroyed its upper storey. Fires play an important role in Marlborough's history. The most notorious one, in April 1653, started in the vicinity of Vincent Head's shop and spread rapidly east and north, destroying 150 shops, houses, and inns all along the High Street and up Kingsbury Street to the Green. The roof of St Mary's Church fell in and the Guild Hall was entirely destroyed. Much of Marlborough was rebuilt within a few years including the Shambles, a row of semi permanent shops along the middle of the High Street where the market is held today. These were finally pulled down in 1812 and hence the amazing width of the street.

THE GREEN
MARLBOROUGH

The charming cottages and houses that form a square around the sloping Green were built on the site of the original Saxon settlement. This lovely open space with its double row of pollarded limes is thus the oldest part of Marlborough. King John's charter of 1204 allowed Marlborough twice weekly markets and these would have been held here until the development of the High Street. The annual sheep fair was held on the Green until 1893.

ST GEORGE'S PRESHUTE

Very little remains of the original Norman church, still less of its Saxon predecessor, but the present building of flint and stone largely dating from 1854 is most attractive and worth investigation. There are a couple of interesting brasses and tablets and an incredible black marble 13th century font which is thought to have been brought from the chapel in Marlborough Castle when it became derelict. Anyone interested in the history of this very old parish and Marlborough itself should read the Wiltshire Library reprint of the Marlborough and Preshute section of the *Victoria History of Wiltshire.*

THE OLD MILL MANTON

Corn and cloth mills are found all along the Kennet valley, some of them mentioned in Domesday and a few like Town Mill, first mentioned in 1204 when given by King John to Nicholas Barfleur, only falling into disuse this century. That intrepid traveller Celia Fiennes was impressed with the view of Marlborough from Granham Hill 'with its two church towers, its very large streete and the Kennet turning many mills.' There is a record of a mill at Manton in 1249 and the present 18th century mill only ceased working in 1933.

THE KENNET MARLBOROUGH

From Silbury to Hungerford the Kennet is now confined to its fixed channel but prior to this century much of this valley was farmed as water meadows. When the river does flood today the outlines of the intricate system of drains, carriers and sluices is clearly visible. The skilled 'drowners' would carefully flood the meadows in the autumn and again in late winter to fertilize and consolidate the ground and to keep it frost free. In April sheep would graze the first crop of young grass, and then, following a quick flooding, a rich crop of hay would be harvested. Cattle would then graze the meadows until the whole programme was started again around Michaelmas. Today a quick squirt of fertilizer has a similar effect.

SHEEP AND SHEPHERDING

Sheep and shepherds have populated the Downs around Marlborough for hundreds of years and although Wiltshire's own horned sheep survive only as a 'rare breed' large flocks of cross breds remain an important part of local agriculture. W.H. Hudson in his classic book on rural Wiltshire, *A Shepherd's Life,* quotes the old shepherd Caleb Bawcombe 'I don't say that I want to live my life again, because 'twould be sinful. We must take what is sent. But if 'twas offered to me and I was told to choose my work, I'd say, give me my Wiltshire Downs again and let me be a shepherd there all my life long.'

THE KENNET
MILDENHALL

The Roman town of Cunetio lay to the south-east of Mildenhall (pronounced locally as 'Minal') and recent extensive excavations prove that it must have been a settlement of some importance. The Roman road to Bath is ill defined until west of Marlborough but the one north to Wanborough and south to Old Sarum through the Savernake is clearly visible. St John Baptist seen here across the river is a fine village church of many periods with magnificent Gothick furnishings provided by the same Charles Francis responsible for the school building.

THE OLD SCHOOL
MILDENHALL

An eccentrically flamboyant design for a school built in 1823 as a result of a generous bequest by the rector Charles Francis. It has now been converted into a private house.

RACEHORSES MANTON

The Marlborough Downs seem criss-crossed with gallops such is the number of racing stables in the area. Famous names from the past like Fred Darling, Alec Taylor, George Todd, Bob Turnell and Jeremy Tree are matched today by the equally successful Roger Charlton, Peter Chapple-Hyam, Peter Makin and a little to the south, Richard Hannon. For several centuries there were race meetings on Marlborough Common and just recently the superbly sited racecourse below Barbury Castle has once again been used for Point-to-Point racing.

THE OLD STABLES MANTON

Manton House has always been a large training establishment with an amazing range of downland turf gallops and a record of success to match. This yard in its Victorian heyday under Alec Taylor was considered palatial. But the money poured into the 2,300 acre estate by Robert Sangster in recent years has transformed the place and it now includes eleven separate gallops, three stable yards and six miles of private roads. A courageous investment fully justified by results.

LOCKERIDGE DENE

A natural deposit of sarsen stones, known as Grey Wethers because of their resemblance to sheep, lie along the valley floor. Since Neolithic times this extremely hard sand stone has been used for building purposes in stone circles, burial chambers, churches and as masonry in cottages. Such was the depradation on these outcrops earlier this century the National Trust stepped in and acquired land to preserve the stones in their natural setting.

WEST WOODS

Fortunately criss-crossed with rights of way so that access is not a problem, West Woods is renowned for its bluebells and wild daffodils in spring but at any season of the year including winter it is perfect walking country. A good map is recommended as the wood which was originally part of the Savernake still extends to 600 acres. The Wansdyke passes through the wood to the south and east and further to the south west, although beyond the reach of the footpath, lies the abandoned medieval village of Shaw.

FYFIELD DOWN

The Nature Reserve can be reached from either Rockley, Avebury, Overton Down or Fyfield on the A4. This extensive area of natural downland untouched by modern farming methods includes woodlands and a valley strewn with sarsen stones. Whilst serious botanists and ornithologists will find plenty to enthuse about it is also an ideal place for family walks and summer picnics. The old Bath-London road used to pass over Fyfield Down just behind the beech trees on its way from Avebury to Marlborough.

DEVIL'S DEN CLATFORD BOTTOM

All that remains of a late Neolithic long barrow originally 230 feet long. The surviving stone chamber with its massive three foot thick capstone looks much as it did in William Stukeley's drawing of 1723. However in truth it was re-erected in 1921. Unusually for this type of barrow, it is in a valley and not set on the skyline. A couple of miles to the south west lies the East Kennett Long Barrow, covered with trees, unexcavated and almost certainly intact. It is on private land and there is no right of way to it.

ST MICHAEL'S WEST OVERTON

The elegant tower of St Michael's, West Overton always seems to catch the eye of drivers on the A4. The church is not as old as it may seem having been largely rebuilt in 1878 but many of the features of the earlier churches on the site have been incorporated. Overton itself was first recorded in the 10th century as Uferantune when it was held by the Abbess of Wilton.

GREY WETHERS PICKLEDEAN

Grey Wethers on National Trust land just north of the A4 near Fyfield. In the church-yard there is a headstone marking the grave of Edward Free, one of a group of stonemasons who came to the area from Buckinghamshire in 1850 to work the sarsen stones. They had perfected the difficult art of splitting the stone into blocks and demand from as far as Bristol kept them in work. But the personal cost was high as most of them died in their forties from silicosis and, no doubt, the rigours of working exposed on the downs in all weathers.

AVEBURY

It is difficult to get a complete view of the Avebury Circles, excepting of course from the air, and on that score Stonehenge may have the edge but the sheer size and scope of Avebury seldom fails to impress. Aubrey said of it to King Charles II that it "did as much excel Stonehenge as a cathedral does a parish church." Since Aubrey's time sadly many of the stones have disappeared - their sites being marked by concrete posts. The village expanded and many houses were constructed from broken sarsens. In the 20th century the wanton destruction of the stones and Circles ceased only for the village itself to be under threat as moves were made by the new owner, Alexander Keiller, to demolish houses within the Circles. Stones which had been buried since the 14th century were exhumed and the Avebury we see today reconstructed. Avebury owes much to Aubrey and Stukeley who so capably chronicled the past and to Alexander Keiller whose generosity and enthusiasm made reconstruction possible.

AVEBURY MANOR

Thankfully the National Trust now owns this famous Tudor manor and it is to be hoped that, after their recent trials and tribulations, the house and grounds will be fully restored. The Alexander Keiller Museum in the old stable block tells the story of the Windmill Hill people as well as the excavation history of the Avebury Circles, and nearby the huge 17th century Great Barn houses the museum of the Wiltshire Folk Life Society. Those in need of refreshment should consider the excellent Stones restaurant adjacent to the Great Barn.

AVEBURY

'Avebury is a haunting place to see at all times and in all weathers, but most impressive of all on a still moonlight night, when it seems to be peopled with ghosts and the old church and cottages of the village seem new and insignificant.'

Sir John Betjeman

AVEBURY

For some reason possibly connected with the local Benedictine Priory's intolerance with their pagan connections as many as fifteen stones in the Great Circle and others in the Avenue were buried in medieval times. Gruesome evidence for this came to light with the discovery of Edward I coins and a pair of scissors and tools found alongside a body crushed beneath a buried stone. It seems likely that the barber-surgeon was buried by its premature fall into the pit he was helping to dig. Despite Alexander Keiller's work it seems possible that there are more stones waiting to be unearthed.

AVEBURY

There are numerous guide books to ancient Avebury but few give much space to the history of the village and its people. The population living in the High Street has sharply declined since Victorian times when 300 people lived there. Many of the houses have been demolished. As in most villages the church and its graveyard tell much of the story. There is an excellent inexpensive local guide to the whole history of Avebury, including the village, by Michael Pitts, entitled *Footprints Through Avebury.*

ST JAMES' CHURCH AVEBURY

St James' Church grew in medieval times to match the needs of its parish and consequently is an amalgam of styles from Saxon to late Tudor. Perhaps its most important feature is the magnificent rood loft and screen - one of very few to survive the Reformation. This was discovered during 19th century restoration work hidden behind a false wall of lath and plaster against the east wall of the nave, and repainted in its bright original colours. Much of the rood screen is Victorian but the loft with its candle holders is entirely original. Unfortunately there is no trace of the Great Rood itself - a large painted wooden image of Christ on the cross. Most rood lofts, notably at Preshute, did not survive reformation zeal.

AVEBURY TRUSLOE MANOR

In the 16th century there was great rivalry between the owners of this estate and that of Avebury Manor as to who owned the manorial rights. Sir James Mervyn of Avebury Manor eventually succeeded and the Truslowe family had to admit defeat including the loss of the dovecote which they had built! Several centuries later descendants of the Truslowe family in New York sent money for the choir stalls in the church to be constructed out of the original Truslowe family pew.

SILBURY HILL

An enigma best viewed from some distance, not necessarily the A4 layby. Neolithic certainly, but three excavations using a shaft through the centre from the top in 1776 and tunnels from the sides in 1848 and 1968 have yielded few answers but a profound respect for the building skills of prehistoric man and the knowledge that the first turves were dug in August nearly 5,000 years ago. The bodies of ants found present under the huge weight of chalk provide this evidence. Legends and theories abound but Silbury remains a wonderful mystery.

WAGGON AND HORSES BECKHAMPTON

A.G. Bradley in his *Roundabout Wiltshire* written in 1907 says 'apart from a rugged coaching inn Beckhampton harbours few people but those devoted to the training of the thoroughbred and the cult of the greyhound.' Little has changed - horses and greyhounds can be seen on the Beckhampton gallops most days. Charles Dickens must have stayed here because he used it in a story which appears in *The Pickwick Papers*. Certainly this inn would have been a welcome sight to drovers and coachmen struggling up the long haul from Calne across one of the wildest stretches of the Bath road. The inn had its own stables, smithy and land, marked by Scots pines, where the drovers could rest their cattle overnight.

CHERHILL DOWN

Visible for miles the slender Lansdowne obelisk erected in 1845 by the third Marquess to commemorate his ancestor Sir William Petty, the 17th century economist. To the left a white horse cut in 1780 by Dr Allsop of Calne. He is said to have marked out the shape with flags and then retreated to a spot where he could fine tune the design by bellowing instructions through a megaphone to his helpers. The result is rather more lively than some other Wiltshire white horses. The eye of the horse some four feet across was filled with bottles embedded upside down to reflect the light. As with other chalk figures there were initial problems following heavy rain but this was helped by cutting a narrow trench above to deflect the streams.

THE WANSDYKE

The Wiltshire section of the Wansdyke runs from Morgan's Hill to the edge of the Savernake. The western section crossing the Devizes road at Shepherd's Shore is massively built with a ditch on the north side. It must originally have had a defensive purpose but as it progresses eastwards through West Woods and the Savernake it is less substantial and perhaps was treated more as a boundary marker. It is suggested that it was raised in the late 6th century as a defensive border between the Saxons of Wiltshire and those of the Thames valley. The only original gap in its whole length is at Red Shore above Alton Priors where the Ridgeway cuts through it on its way south.

THE WANSDYKE

On a sunny clear day walking the Wansdyke has much to recommend it. There is a public right-of-way along its most impressive section from Morgan's Hill to the Lockeridge-Alton Priors road, followed by a short detour along the Wansdyke Path skirting the deserted village of Shaw and back to the Wansdyke itself running through West Woods. The final section just before the Savernake is across private land.

CHERHILL DOWN

A wild and empty countryside much feared by travellers in the past on account of the highwaymen who preyed not only on the rich on the Bath road but local people returning from market. A Charles Taylor was convicted in 1743 at the Wiltshire Assizes for relieving an Ogbourne farmer of seventy pounds. The notorious Cherhill gang are said to have stripped naked before attacking their victims at night - one way of not being recognised! Gibbets were erected at Beckhampton and on Morgan's Hill and put to use.

STUBBLE BURNING

Few people who have suffered the fall out of ash and debris regret the banning of straw burning, but the sight and sound of the flames thrastling across the stubble and the subsequent pall of smoke hanging in the autumn sky is not easily forgotten. Conservationists may well be correct but the cost to agriculture remains to be seen.

WEST KENNETT LONG BARROW

The finest example of a chambered long barrow in Wiltshire over 340 feet long and 75 feet wide. Like its near neighbour the East Kennett Long Barrow which has never been excavated it predates Silbury Hill, the Sanctuary and the Avebury Circles and is contemporary with the settlement on Windmill Hill. It was finally sealed with the five great stones after a thousand years of use in approximately 2,500 BC. Can one conceive of a 20th century building lasting a thousand years let alone being used for a single purpose throughout the period?

WEST KENNETT LONG BARROW

Fortunately the excavation which revealed the side chambers earlier this century was done by professionals. Years earlier a Marlborough doctor, Robert Toope, wrote to John Aubrey describing how he had dug into the barrow to obtain human bones to make 'a noble medicine that relieved many of my distressed neighbours.' Again in 1858 John Thurnam cleared a section of the main passage to satisfy his interest in collecting skulls.

URCHFONT

A village with many attractive houses from the 16th century onwards including Urchfont Manor enthusiastically described by Pevsner as one of the finest in Wiltshire. Here across the village pond with its ducks and imposing cedar is Manor Farmhouse. Behind it, approached on the right, is St. Michael's Church. It is recorded that its beautiful lierne-vaulted chancel - a rarity in a parish church - was created in the early 14th century at the insistence of the Bishop of Salisbury who was displeased with St Mary's Nunnery in Winchester who had allowed the church to become dilapidated. A sobering note in the history of the church records the martyrdom in 1523 in Devizes of an Urchfont tailor John Bent for denying the doctrine of transubstantiation.

URCHFONT

The decline of the village shop has seemed inexorable but happily here it survives in the guise of a successful small butchers shop. Despite the attractions of nearby Devizes it flourishes.

OLD POST OFFICE HORTON

Three would surely be a crowd in here! Sadly the gradual demise of the village shop seems irreversible. The local historian John Chandler in his excellent history of *The Vale of Pewsey* takes as an example the shoe trade. He shows that in 1895 there was a choice of 44 shoemakers and menders in the Vale, in 1935 just 14 and in 1990 no choice but to go into the local town. In contrast the vigorous local defence of village schools in recent years seems to have stemmed the tide of closures.

ROUNDWAY

On the western edge of the area covered in this book Oliver's Castle on the top of Roundway has commanding views to the south and west. Below it in 1643 the Royalist forces under Lord Wilmot scored a famous cavalry victory over the parliamentary army commanded by Sir William Waller who fled the field leaving his men to surrender.

ST MARY'S CHURCH
BISHOP'S CANNINGS

A magnificent cruciform church with central tower and spire and little steeple in one corner visible for miles along the Pewsey Vale. Before visiting the church it is advisable to ascertain whether it is locked against vandalism and also worth reading Pevsner's enthusiastic description of the building. Like Potterne it is considerably grander than its locality might suggest, the reason being it was built by the Bishop of Salisbury on his estate.

BOX PEW
ST MARY'S CHURCH

A 17th century penitential seat with an enormous outstretched hand bearing dire warnings in Latin presumably to put the fear of damnation into the beholder. Ida Gandy, daughter of the vicar of St Mary's, wrote in 1929 a charming description of her early childhood spent in this then remote and secluded village in *A Wiltshire Childhood*. This book is again in print as is her excellent history of Aldbourne, *The Heart of a Village*.

ALL SAINTS
MARDEN

A gem of a village church with this lovely south doorway and inside a fine Norman chancel arch slightly flattened due to the settlement of the building whose poor foundations have necessitated several rebuilding phases. The pulpit is Jacobean and there is modern stained glass well worth seeing. An attractive feature of the street is the happy mixture of well kept hedges and fine garden walls, some thatched.

STOKE FARM
BEECHINGSTOKE

Throughout the Vale of Pewsey it is noticeable how often the farmhouses were built within the villages, on the main street and often quite close together, and not as elsewhere in the middle of their farms. Whilst the older houses, for example at Wilsford, were timber-framed and thatched, in the 18th and 19th centuries, with the coming of the canal and the development of local brickworks, most were built of brick and some had slate roofs.

THE TIMBERS
WILSFORD

In 1841 parish records reveal a population of 304, now it is less than 100 and Wilsford no longer has any shops or a school. Small it may be but along its street between the Manor and Wilsford House can be seen some of the oldest thatched cottages in the Vale - notably the Malthouse and No.18 which is medieval and extends to four cruck trusses. The cottage seen here has been carefully restored to reveal this intricate brickwork which was hidden for years behind grey rendering. The church from where this photograph was taken is also worthy of mention. It dates back to the 12th century and has been altered and restored in most centuries since reflecting the history of the village. At one time there was a chapel on the north side which was used as a schoolroom until 1848 and then as a bakery. It was demolished in 1959.

VINEYARD
VALE OF PEWSEY

Agriculture in the fertile Vale of Pewsey covers most crops but there is only one vineyard. Despite the vagaries of our summer and a hostile tax regime English wine is gradually finding its way onto the wine merchants' shelves. Perhaps in Norman times the climate was more suitable as there is mention in Domesday of a vineyard at Wilcot.

DAFFODILS WOODBOROUGH

This sea of daffodils to be followed by tulips, rivals any bulb field in Holland. The firm of nurserymen Walter Ware has been in existence in Bath since 1883. They used the fields in Woodborough as trial grounds for growing new varieties of daffodils and tulips and at the instigation of the famous plantswoman Ellen Willmott they first grew here the Fortune strain of daffodil. Nowadays the Bath nursery is under different management and Woodborough is the principal nursery. Daffodils, strawberries, raspberries and sweetcorn are grown for the pick-your-own market.

PLOUGHING VALE OF PEWSEY

Cobbett's 'land of promise' has long been recognised as highly fertile and productive but the Vale has not escaped the general farming trend towards the use of artificial fertilizers and pesticides. The exception, and a very successful one, is Rushall farm where Barry Wookey has pioneered a return to organic farming by gradually converting his large acreage to chemical-free cultivation. His book, *Rushall, the Story of an Organic Farm* is a brilliant polemic on behalf of the organic movement and shows how it is possible to be efficient, profitable and organic and retain your enthusiasm for farming and wildlife. The mill at Rushall grinds their wholemeal flour and the bakery operates on Tuesday and Friday. Their bread and other organic products are on sale there or can be bought in Marlborough at Mackintosh's delicatessen in the High Street.

BARGE INN
HONEYSTREET

This welcoming canalside pub is sadly all that remains of a once thriving industrial community. The approach by road is through a sawmill yard which is now independent of the canal. In the boom years the wharf, built in 1811, was the distribution point for building materials and coal for the whole area and exported to Bristol farm produce and sarsen stone from the Marlborough Downs. The wharf was owned by Robbins, Lane and Pinnegar who also built 'Kennet' barges and ran a timber yard. They fought a long battle with the railway but the gradual decline of the condition of the canal itself finally defeated them in the 1940s. Now that much of the canal is open again barges can once more call at the inn.

WHITE HORSE
ALTON BARNES

An enthusiastic local farmer, also responsible for a smaller horse on Pewsey Down, had a little difficulty in completing this landmark as his original contractor, an itinerant painter, absconded with the substantial £20 advance fee! It was completed in 1812 on the side of Milk Hill which is now within the Pewsey Down Nature Reserve and so access is along the footpath from Adam's Grave or up the steep hill from Alton Barnes. Perhaps a brief mention should be made of another form of art in the landscape - man made or not - corn circles. Spectacular examples have appeared around Avebury and in the fields below this White Horse near the Workway Drove.

KNAP HILL

The Pewsey Downs National Nature Reserve extends along the south escarpment of the down from Knap Hill towards Tan Hill. Access is best from the car park on the top of the hill on the Marlborough/Alton Barnes road. The area includes the site of the Neolithic long barrow known as Adam's Grave and the White Horse carved on the side of Milk Hill. The turf has never been ploughed, is still grazed by sheep and is therefore rich in many rare chalkland plants. A field guide to wild flowers and butterflies is recommended and a pair of good binoculars to enjoy both the fabulous views across the Vale and to identify the increasing number of birds of prey.

ALTON PRIORS

The view from Walkers Hill showing the two tiny villages almost as one with the Alton Priors church in the fields and the older Saxon church of Alton Barnes almost hidden by the trees. St Mary's is worth visiting to see its gallery and timbered roof with its tie-beams although the now redundant Alton Priors church is better known due to its association with Augustus and Maria Hare. Looking now across this small agricultural community it is hard to appreciate how much bigger and more important these two parishes were in earlier times. There is an excellent short history available in St Mary's.

WORKWAY DROVE

In Richard Jefferies' era gypsies or 'gips' as he called them were often seen camped in the old green lanes covering the Downs. There is a Gypsy Lane leading up to Barbury Castle from the Swindon road. He mentions them in his *Amateur Poacher* commenting on their incredible hardiness and describes their 'tents formed by thrusting the ends of long tent rods like half-hoops into the turf, looked dark like the canvas of a barge.' The family pictured here is on the old Workway Drove which climbs up the side of Knap Hill towards the Wansdyke and Tan Hill. Gypsies played an important role in the Tan Hill Fair providing many of the sideshows and presumably dealing in horses. The last fair was held in 1932.

WOODBOROUGH HILL

Woodborough Hill and its near neighbour the conical shaped Picked Hill rise up as chalk outcrops from the floor of the Vale. Hilltops seem significant in local history from the earliest times well into the 19th century as sites for fairs, social gatherings and religious festivals. Silbury Hill was climbed on Palm Sunday as was Martinsell on the top of which local people held a sports day involving boys sliding down its steepest slopes on horse skulls. Picked Hill was climbed on Good Friday and the most famous fair of all which attracted huge crowds was the St Anne's Fair on Tan Hill in early August. It is said that fires were lit before dawn to guide people to the site. Today these hilltops are largely deserted although of course they attract walkers and sometimes when the angle of descent is suitable hang gliders can be seen.

CHISENBURY PRIORY

Travelling south from Upavon leave the busy A345 at Enford cross the river and return on the quiet parallel road. The Priory is not visible from the road but a footpath curls behind it and this lovely house is revealed. In stark contrast is Chisenbury Warren a couple of miles to the east high on the downs. It can be reached along another footpath from Littlecott near the bridge at Enford. In this long abandoned valley there was a Romano-British settlement and the street, 400 yards long, clearly shows the position of 80 houses.

THE AVON CHISENBURY

The Vale of Pewsey is drained by the two upper branches of the Avon which meet just above Upavon to flow south along this valley to Salisbury. This is as far south as the scope of this book allows but mention must be made of the church of All Saints at Enford. It unfortunately suffered some damage to the nave when the spire collapsed in 1817 but it is an important church with a long history and well worth a visit. It is usually locked but the key is readily available. The substantial lychgate is a fine memorial to parishioners who died in the two world wars.

OAK FARM COTTAGE WILCOT

An arresting sight on the road from Alton Barnes to Wilcot, there are hundreds of similar thatched cottages in the area but few can rival this one's luxuriant bonnet of creeper! In Wilcot itself there is more thatch but it is the Green with its matching cottages evenly spaced along its three sides that catches the eye. To make way for the building of Stowell Lodge and its park in 1813 the houses in East Stowell were demolished and the inhabitants rehoused in this model estate village. The arbitrary destruction of a whole community seems harsh but in fact such was the state of rural housing in the early 19th century it must have been an improvement. A similar row of perfectly matching cottages was built at the same time to accommodate workers at the Chilton Lodge estate at Leverton.

HOLY CROSS CHURCH WILCOT

The oldest part of the village is a little away from the Green and clusters closely around Holy Cross Church. Domesday mentions the existence of a new church, a magnificent mansion and a good vineyard. It is very rare for a private house to be specifically mentioned in Domesday so it must have been especially significant. The present manor is largely 18th century. The church was gutted by a fire in 1878, said to have been caused by sparks from the manor's chimney, but there survives in the chancel wall an Elizabethan monument to John Berwick recording that his daughter married Sir Thomas Wroughton. Three hundred years later the Wroughton family were still involved in the church - a Colonel Wroughton provided a new chancel in 1825.

WINDPUMP
PEWSEY VALE

Quite common on the Downs and in the Vale a few years ago, there's one near the abandoned village of Snap above Aldbourne, but nowadays seldom seen and none are thought still to be working. Perhaps one day there will be a wind farm on Hackpen or Liddington? Another man-made feature of the local landscape which thankfully has never had to be put to the test is the line of pill-boxes and tank traps dotted along the canal from Devizes to Newbury. This marked an inland line of defence known as the 'Blue Line' designed to stop Hitler's panzers and the sturdy buildings are quite likely to outlive their grander forebears, the Martello towers on the Kent coast built to repel Napoleon.

HARVESTING
PEWSEY VALE

Everyone seems to have a view on the rights and wrongs of modern farming methods - perhaps it was always so - but the industry is burdened with more than its fair share of ill-informed criticism. The one undeniable fact is that whilst access to the countryside is ever more easy less and less people are actually earning their living on the land. If the great agrarian agitator William Cobbett could retrace his steps across the Marlborough countryside he would be amazed at how few people he could see in the fields especially at harvest time. Complaints about government policy would not be slow in coming but surely he would still consider much of it 'a land of promise'.

HUISH

A remote hamlet, just west of Oare, under the escarpment of Huish Hill, with an old rectory and a charming simple church dating from the 18th and 19th century but built on the foundations of a larger church which suggests that the village was more important in medieval times. On a sunny day the views from the church porch across the lightly wooded vale to the south and along the edge of the downs to Martinsell in the east are spectacular and worth a visit in themselves.

DRAYCOTT HILL

Earthworks, tumuli, Neolithic camps, backed by the great Wansdyke itself appear all along these hills from Martinsell in the east to Draycott, Walkers and Tan Hill in the west. But since Saxon times very few people have lived up on these hills. Probably the last settlement of any size was the village of Shaw less than a mile north of Draycott Hill. Mentioned in Domesday it was abandoned some time before the end of the 15th century. Unlike Snap above Aldbourne there is little written evidence to explain its demise. Perhaps it was as a result of the Plague, change in agricultural practices or merely the hardship of life without a local source of water.

OARE HOUSE LODGE

Clematis montana cascades over the lodge standing beside the lime tree avenue which leads from the village street up to Oare House. Oare House and Rainscombe House are rightly much admired for the splendour of their design and setting but Teulon's red and blue brick church built in 1857 is another matter. It is amusing to read Pevsner's partial retraction of his initial view that 'this church is the ugliest in Wiltshire.' Later editions consider 'in Teulon's work this kind of ugliness is an asset.'

OARE HOUSE

To get the best all round view of this lovely house and its grounds take the minor road to Huish, grasp the opportunity to visit the church, then go on to Draycot FitzPayne and back to Oare turning left just before the main road. This passes in front of the house between the lime avenue and the fine wrought iron gates and railings. The house was built in 1740 for a London wine-merchant and was considerably enlarged in 1921 by Clough Williams-Ellis who added two symmetrical wings. The garden is well worth a visit being open occasionally under the National Gardens scheme.

EARTHWORKS
HUISH HILL

All along the side of Huish Hill and Oare Hill these earthworks appear, presumably defensive in origin, although this one is said to have been used subsequently as a drove road up from the Vale. Only the most famous drove roads like the Ridgeway or the Workway Drove are marked on modern maps, but records show that in the 18th and 19th centuries when large movements of cattle and sheep were necessary to feed the growing cities hundreds of thousands of animals were driven at about 10 miles a day along these green roads which at times exceeded a mile in width as they crossed the open downs. Dewponds and drover inns like the Waggon and Horses at Beckhampton, formerly known as The Bear, where the cattle and sheep could be 'stanced' at night were essential - turnpike roads where tolls were levied were avoided!

MARTINSELL HILL

Crowned by the Giant's Grave, Martinsell forms the east side of the great horseshoe curve of Rainscombe. The setting of Rainscombe House must be one of the most beautiful in England. The stiff walk up from Oare through the earthworks on Huish Hill, across the Marlborough road, on the Tan Hill way and back along the ridge of Martinsell is not for the faint hearted, but the views in every direction are impressive. The footpath descends the hillside and returns to Oare along the lane leading to West Wick. This is Tedworth country and local histories record the eccentricities of the famous 19th century hunting squire Assheton Smith who among other exploits rode with his hounds down the precipitous side of Martinsell. His long suffering huntsman, George Carter, who in his day was almost as famous as his master, is buried at Milton as is another hunting character, Parson Gale.

ST JOHN BAPTIST
PEWSEY

The Saxon settlement of Pevisigge lay between the river and the area of higher ground on which this Norman church was subsequently built. Much of the medieval building remains although extensive restoration was carried out in the l9th century. In the last few years much time and effort has been expended in improving what has to be said was a rather gloomy interior. It is surprising what modern lighting and an amazing collection of brightly coloured hassocks can do to make a church welcoming and alive.

BALL CORNER
PEWSEY

A well preserved pair of timber-framed thatched cottages, the one on the left being of cruck construction and on the right box-framed. This is one of the earliest and simplest ways of building using a matching pair of timbers - ideally two halves of the same tree - as frames tied at the top and braced across the middle. One advantage of this method is that the cottage can be extended by adding another pair of crucks. The infill can be either wattle and daub or brick.

BRIDGE COTTAGES, PEWSEY

These pretty cottages in the centre of the village facing King Alfred somehow reflect the history of Pewsey. Whilst it has always been the capital of the Vale it never acquired the all important market charter which often led to urban status in earlier times. Pewsey has remained a busy large village serving a local population and, unlike Marlborough, it still has the great advantage of a railway station with a fast service to London.

KING ALFRED PEWSEY

King Alfred is honoured with statues throughout Wessex, notably in Winchester and Wantage but Pewsey does have some claim to him in that it formed part of his personal estates. This statue was erected to commemorate the coronation of George V - Pewsey likes to mark such occasions - the white horse to the south of the town was recut in 1937 to mark George VI's coronation.

CANAL HOUSE
PEWSEY WHARF

Tradition has it that this section of the canal was built by French prisoners-of-war which probably explains how the local inn was named the French Horn. The walk west along the towpath past Stowell Park on the right and Wilcot is nearly four miles and includes some of the prettiest scenes of the whole canal. Note how the canal widens on the other side of Wilcot to form a narrow lake ending at Ladies Bridge. Apparently Lady Wroughton, owner of Wilcot Manor insisted that if the canal was to cross her land in 1808 this ornamental lake and bridge should be constructed. It is now a haven for wildlife.

PLEASE
DO NOT INJURE
A man of kindness to his beast is kind
A brutal action shows a brutal mind
Remember He who made thee made the brute
Who gave thee speech and reason formed him mute
He can't complain, but God's all-seeing eye
Beholds thy cruelty and hears his cry
He was designed thy servant, not thy drudge
Remember He who made thee is thy judge

FORD BROOK
PEWSEY

This gentle appeal for kindness to horses formerly stood by the horse trough on the Pewsey/Marlborough road below Haybrook House. A few local residents can still remember carters using the trough to water their horses.

STIBB GREEN BURBAGE

The inhabitants of Burbage and Stibb Green have long sought a bypass to relieve traffic congestion in the straight mile long village street. Now at last they have one and the character of the village is changing. In the almost total absence of traffic crossing the street is no longer a risky undertaking but by the same token many fewer passing cars has meant the closure of shops and pubs. Now there is a wise move to advertise the many services the village has to offer on hoardings at either end of the village.

PLOUGHING MATCH EASTON ROYAL

On Monday 28th August 1826 William Cobbett on one of his famous rural rides paused on Milton Hill and later recorded 'I never before saw anything to please me like this valley of the Avon. I sat upon my horse, and looked over Milton and Easton and Pewsey for half an hour, though I had not breakfasted. Great as my expectations had been, they were more than fulfilled. I delight in this sort of country. Villages, hamlets, large farms, towers, steeples, fields, meadows, orchards and very fine timber-trees, scattered all over the valley.' One cannot help speculating on what Cobbett might have to say today about modern agriculture and the Common Market - his views would no doubt be as trenchant as those expressed in his *Rural Rides*.

ROUGH DOWN MARLBOROUGH

'In the arms of the wind, vast bundles of mist are borne against the hill; they widen and slip, and lengthen, drawing out; the wind works quickly with moist colours ready and a wide brush laying broadly. Colour comes up in the wind; the thin mist disappears, drunk up in the grass and trees, and the air is full of blue behind the vapour. Blue sky at the far horizon - rich deep blue overhead - a dark-brown blue deep yonder in the gorge among the trees. I feel a sense of blue colour as I face the strong breeze; the vibration and blow of its force answer to that hue, the sound of the swinging branches and the rush-rush in the grass is azure in its note; it is wind-blue, not the night-blue, or heaven-blue, a colour of air.'
Richard Jefferies *Field and Hedgerow*

SAVERNAKE FOREST

'Far as the eye can see extends an avenue of beech, passing right through the forest. The tall, smooth trunks rise up to a great height, and then branch overhead, looking like the roof of a Gothic cathedral. The growth is so regular and so perfect that the comparison springs unbidden to the lip, and here, if anywhere, that order of architecture might have taken its inspiration. There is a continuous Gothic arch of green for miles, beneath which one may drive or walk, as in the aisles of a forest abbey.'
Richard Jefferies *The Hills and the Vale*

SAVERNAKE FOREST

When it was a royal hunting preserve of the Norman kings the forest stretched from Hungerford to the other side of West Woods. The Seymour family were the hereditary Wardens and at the height of their power during the minority of Edward VI they acquired ownership of the forest. During the 18th century the Wardens planted huge numbers of oaks and beeches and it was these trees that Richard Jefferies saw in their prime. There was another period of planting before the First World War. The Grand Avenue must have been a fabulous sight. Sadly much of it is now decayed and only brief stretches give any idea of its former glory. Nevertheless natural regeneration is being allowed to take place and whilst the formality of the original planting cannot be recreated the forest is very much alive and well.

CADLEY

A small hamlet on the edge of the Savernake straddling the Marlborough/Burbage road. The only public footpath in the whole forest runs from Cadley church to the road just above the hospital. In the three weeks before Christmas the Forestry Commission offer a really excellent choice of good trees of all sizes. The route into the forest is signposted in Cadley.

SAVERNAKE FOREST

In 1939 management of most of the forest passed to the Forestry Commission. Their attitude to the development of the forest has to be primarily commercial but there have been extensive plantings of broad-leaved trees and their stewardship of this great forest is much appreciated by the people of Marlborough. Whilst there is still no legal right-of-way in the Forest access is permitted on foot to most of it and by car down the Grand Avenue. The Commission have also developed the Postern Hill picnic site which includes camping and barbecue facilities. A fascinating *History of the Savernake Forest* and its long line of hereditary Wardens was republished by the Marquess of Ailesbury in 1962 and is still available.

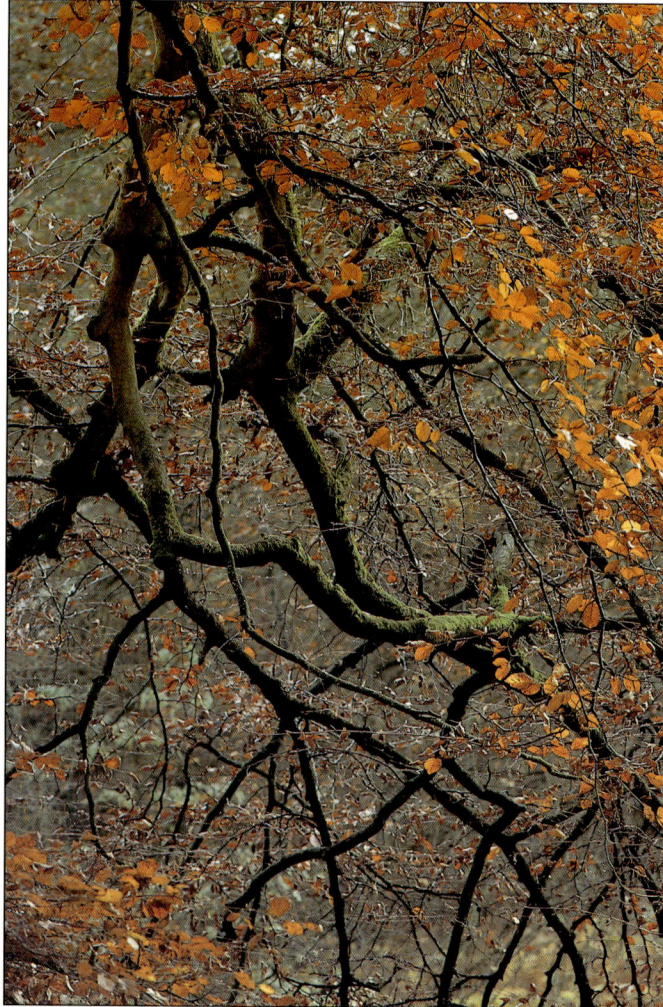

ST KATHERINE'S CHURCH SAVERNAKE

A grand and beautiful estate church built in 1861 by T.H. Wyatt for the second Marchioness of Ailesbury. Light and spacious with graceful stone carvings and a host of interesting Victorian features it is much more than just a mausoleum for the Brudenell-Bruce family. On the other side of the lovely churchyard stands the school which was built at much the same time to educate children on the estate. Fortunately it has withstood the threat of closure and flourishes with a roll of nearly 50.

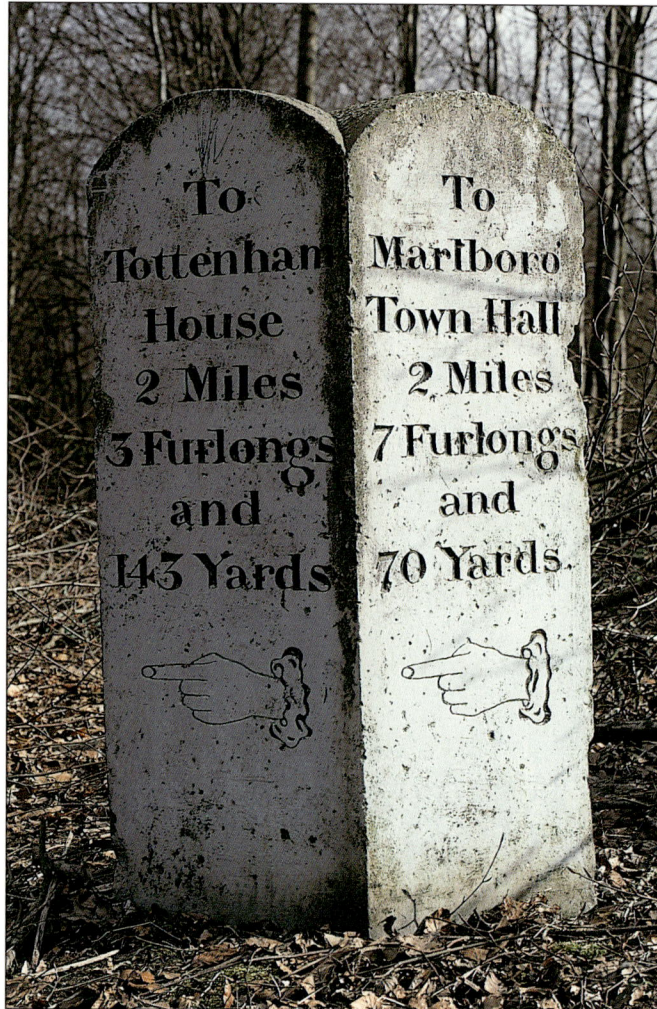

MILESTONE
SAVERNAKE FOREST

A surprising number of milestones still adorn our roads and lanes although it is usually only pedestrians who have the time to read them. This is rather more elaborate than most and is an interesting conceit in that the way indicated to Tottenham House has never been a public right-of-way. The house was formerly the seat of the hereditary Warden of the forest but is now leased to the well-known preparatory school, Hawtreys.

FOUR MILE CLUMP

As the name would suggest this group of trees is four miles from Marlborough. The significance is that this was for centuries the main road to Swindon and was not superseded by the turnpiked Og Valley road until well into the 19th century. The road leaves Rockley at Old Eagle, the site of an old inn, climbs Ogbourne Maizey Down, passes to the east of Barbury Castle and descends to Swindon. It must have been a rugged journey but the route was still being used in the mid-19th century by a horse-drawn coach service between the Castle and Ball Hotel and Swindon. Five milestones mark the way.

THE OGBOURNE VALLEY

The true Ridgeway crosses from Barbury Castle to the north of Liddington and is now a road for some of the way. To avoid this road the Countryside Commission has created its own Ridgeway Path diversion down Smeathe's Ridge to the south of Ogbourne St George, over Round Hill Down, from where this photograph is taken, and north to Liddington Hill where it rejoins the true Ridgeway. Liddington, Barbury and Martinsell are the three great Iron Age hill forts on the Marlborough Downs and as they are sited on the top of the highest hills in the area the views are spectacular. Liddington is very much Richard Jefferies country being 'the hill to which I used to resort' as he recounts in his *Story of My Heart*. He regularly walked the three miles up from his home at Coate, which the M4 makes impossible now, and in fact thought nothing of walking as far as the Savernake.

RIVER OG

The Og is a winterbourne rising near Ogbourne St George and flowing past Ogbourne St Andrew, here, and on under Bay Bridge to join the Kennet at Poulton. The water table has fallen in recent years due in part to drier winters and the river is seldom as full as pictured here. At one time it was dammed to make the King's Great Stew, a fishpond for the inhabitants of Marlborough Castle.

OGBOURNE MAIZEY DOWN

'A barren race they are, the proud poppies, lords of the July field, taking no deep root, but raising up a brilliant blazon of scarlet heraldry out of nothing. They are useless, they are bitter, they are allied to sleep and poison and everlasting night; yet they are forgiven because they are not commonplace. Nothing, no abundance of them, can ever make the poppies common-place. There is genius in them, the genius of colour, and they are saved. Even when they take the room of the corn we must admire them. I wish I could do something more than gaze at all this scarlet and gold and crimson and green, something more than see it, not exactly to drink it or inhale it, but in some way to make it part of me that I might live it.'
Richard Jefferies *Field and Hedgerow*

OGBOURNE MAIZEY MANOR

A Jacobean manor of banded flint and stone with original stone mullions and the date 1636 over the door - the two matching arched windows are Georgian inserts. Sarsen and thatch is very much the theme in the Ogbourne villages and immediately next to this manor there is a range of barns built on massive sarsen stone foundations. This was Bob Turnell's famous racing yard and further up the lane there is more evidence of the importance of the racing industry in this area with Peter Makin's yard on the left and gallops on the hills above Rockley.

HACKPEN HILL

An early morning drive in June along the Broad Hinton road out of Marlborough across the Downs takes some beating. The Downs and trees are at their best, the gallops may well be in use, the views impressive and the traffic light. Park near the top of Hackpen Hill and walk either south along the Ridgeway to Overton Hill and views of Avebury or north to Barbury Castle.

WOODHAM MILL WROUGHTON

Mills played an important role in the history of Wroughton until the end of the 19th century. The streams coming off the chalk provided the power to drive these mills, six are mentioned in Domesday, but with the arrival of the Wilts & Berks canal with the need to use much of this water to maintain levels, a guaranteed constant supply of water was impossible. Steam was introduced and prolonged the life of the mills until the end of the century. This mill, known previously as Pavey's or Baker's, was probably the largest with a substantial millpond and a 26 foot overshot wheel.

THATCHED DUCKS CHISELDON

For centuries the almost universal roofing material in and around Marlborough was thatch. Wheat straw was readily available and labour cheap and a thatched roof was recognised as warm in winter and cool enough in summer. It has the added advantage of not needing gutters or drainpipes. Even the great barn at Wulfhall where it is suggested Henry VIII and Jane Seymour might have held their wedding feast was thatched. Thatching is no longer cheap but happily it is making a comeback and such beautiful villages as Wilcot and Wootton Rivers are not in danger from the ubiquitous concrete tile. It would be interesting to know just how many different animals and birds adorn these roofs.

BARBURY CASTLE

Access by car is from Chiseldon to an enormous car park with information boards, lavatories and an icecream van. It is much visited in summer. Walkers can approach along the Ridgeway from Hackpen Hill or up Smeathe's Ridge from Ogbourne St George. A little to the east on Burderop Down looking across to Liddington there is a sarsen stone memorial to two of Wiltshire's finest authors, Alfred Williams and Richard Jefferies. One plaque reads 'still to find and still to follow, joy in every field and hollow, company in solitude' and the other 'It is eternity now, I am in the midst of it, it is about me in the sunshine.' Richard Jefferies, Alfred Williams, Charles Sorley and John Betjeman are just a few of the writers who have been inspired by the Marlborough Downs.

RAPE ABOVE ALDBOURNE

One of the many 'if onlys' of history took place above Aldbourne during the Civil War. The Earl of Essex with his Parliamentary army of 14,000 men and horses was returning to London having successfully raised the siege of Gloucester. London was without an army and his presence was urgently needed. He skillfully managed to evade the Royalist forces until caught by Prince Rupert's cavalry in the narrow valley leading down to Aldbourne from Snap. Fortunately for Essex the Royalist infantry and guns were miles away and although badly mauled he escaped towards Hungerford. The Royalists eventually forced him to fight at Newbury but the result was inconclusive and he slipped away to London. If the Royalist guns and infantry had also been in place above Aldbourne who knows how the Civil War might have ended?

UPHAM HOUSE

High up on the Downs above Aldbourne lie the remains of two deserted villages and this well preserved Tudor manor. Upper Upham was a medieval village, mentioned in Domesday, and was probably removed to make way for a deer park for John of Gaunt who had a hunting lodge at Upham. The present manor was built by the Goddard family who acquired the land from Henry VIII. The other village, Snap, survived somewhat precariously until the agricultural depression of the 1890s and was finally abandoned in 1905. The footpath from Aldbourne, which eventually crosses the Ridgeway, runs along the village street and the ruins of the houses are clearly discernible. Life must have been hard at the best of times up here and the little valley, not surprisingly, has a melancholy air.

ACROSS THE GREEN
ALDBOURNE

Below the church lies the Green which was once the village Market Place and on which still stands the Market Cross. In the 18th century Aldbourne was famous for the manufacture of bells of all kinds but particularly, church bells. It was from the foundry at Court House above the Green that first the Cor and then the Wells families sent out more than 300 bells to churches throughout Wiltshire. Tradition has it that two bells destined for St Michael's were first turned upside down outside the Blue Boar, seen here across the Green, and filled with beer for a general celebration.

THE OLD MALTHOUSE
ALDBOURNE

Well into the Victorian era malting was a cottage industry and some maltsters would actually do the brewing as well. But with the growth of the large breweries malthouses fell into disuse and became barns or private houses. This one survived, with its weather-cock in the shape of a maltster with his shovel, and acquired fame in 1910 when it was briefly converted into a theatre. A London dramatist who had moved to Aldbourne produced his play 'The Village Wedding' using local talent recruited from the village. Celebrities such as Bernard Shaw claimed to have enjoyed it although admitting to having some difficulty with the local dialect!

RAMSBURY MANOR

For centuries the manor of Ramsbury belonged to the bishops of Salisbury, then in 1552, it passed to the Earl of Pembroke who extended the park on both sides of the river to over a thousand acres, planting huge numbers of oaks. In turn his house was demolished in 1680 to make way for this fine country house built for the successful lawyer Sir William Jones. The lake, the lodge gates and the bridge, from where this photograph was taken, were added in 1776. Since then very little has been altered but the tradition of planting trees has continued and the park is a delight to see.

STITCHCOMBE

Looking north east across the Kennet valley between Mildenhall and Axford. The road to Ramsbury keeps to the north of the river and swings further away up White's Hill skirting the edge of Ramsbury Manor Park. However using a series of footpaths and lanes it is possible to keep close to the river on the south side from Stitchcombe to Ramsbury. This stretch of the river is particularly strong in wildlife and a summer walk here has much to recommend it.

HIGH STREET RAMSBURY

Communications obviously play a vital part in the growth of a village and it is interesting to note how this has affected Ramsbury over the years. It is hard to believe that well into the 18th century this narrow High Street was part of the main road between London and Bristol. However in 1744 the Savernake stretch of the Hungerford/Marlborough road was turnpiked and most of the traffic subsequently avoided 'the miserable waggon track, called the Ramsbury narrow way'. The Kennet and Avon canal was originally planned to pass through Ramsbury but the southern route through Bedwyn and Pewsey was chosen. Likewise the railway never came. In 1846 Swindon was still smaller than Ramsbury.

THE SQUARE RAMSBURY

Until recently an ancient elm stood in the Square. The battle over whether or not to replace it made headline news. But it was really the Building Society whose headquarters was in the Square and who used the elm as its emblem that brought Ramsbury fame. The Society, founded in 1846 by the Rev. Richard Frost was strongly supported by the Non-Conformist element in the village enabling them to buy their own freeholds and assert their independence both of the Manor and the Established Church. The Society remained a local one until the 1960's when it rapidly expanded throughout Wiltshire and beyond until eventually being taken over by the Portman.

HOLY CROSS RAMSBURY

This church was built on the site of the old Saxon Minster in the 13th century, the nave extended and the tower added in the 14th. The Saxon bishopric created in 909 gave the Bishop of Ramsbury jurisdiction over Wiltshire and Berkshire and lasted until 1058 when it merged with Sherborne and finally Old Sarum. The Bishops of Salisbury continued to own the Manor until the Reformation and endeavoured to help the fortunes of the village by granting permission for a weekly market. However the Marlborough merchants petitioned the King who prohibited this competition and Ramsbury had to be content with two annual fairs. The interior of the church is well worth attention having a wealth of interesting furnishings, monuments and the fragments of Saxon crosses. There was great celebration when the Ramsbury bishopric was revived in 1974.

FOUNDRY COTTAGE RAMSBURY

Stephen Osmond was one of several ironfounders to set up in the village in the 19th century. Cobbett on one of his rural rides in 1826 reported Ramsbury to be 'a large apparently miserable village'. This may well have been true then but after the repeal of the Corn Laws prosperity returned to agriculture and Ramsbury enjoyed several decades of good years until the agricultural depression of the 1890's. Threshing machines and steam engines were in demand and Osmond's foundry in the Newtown Road was in business until the 1920's.

ST MARTIN CHISBURY

Standing just inside the east entrance of Chisbury Iron Age hillfort is this exquisite ruined chapel. Built of flint and thatched, its windows still bear the remains of 13th century tracery. It was originally attached to the church in Great Bedwyn but like many chapels-of-ease it was abandoned after the Reformation. It survived as a farm building and is on private land, but access is permitted up the track leading off the Chisbury/Little Bedwyn road.

WILTON WINDMILL

Working until the 1920's and fully restored by the Wiltshire Historic Buildings Trust in the 1970's it has recently suffered some damage but it is once again in working order and open to the public on Sundays and bank holidays in the summer.

LITTLE BEDWYN

The canal and railway run side-by-side through Little Bedwyn. The canal came first in 1810 being dug by navvies with pick, shovel and barrow, each moving 12 cubic yards a day. The next generation brought the railway and from the 1840's the tonnage carried on the Kennet and Avon canal, which had peaked at 360,000 tons, declined until closure in the 1940's. Now after years of hard work the canal is once again fully operational and a valuable public amenity. The history of the canal and the restoration work are well displayed at the Canal Trust Centre Museum on Devizes Wharf.

DURLEY

Marlborough no longer has a railway but it is still possible to trace the line of the Midland and South Western Junction Railway from Swindon to the old Savernake Station, near Durley. North of Marlborough the old track has now been converted into a cycleway as far as Chiseldon. South of Marlborough it is rather more confusing as a second track is also visible because, for some fifty years, there were two separate railway lines under different management between Marlborough and Savernake Station. Railway buffs should consult *The Marlborough Branch* by Kevin Robertson and David Abbott and *Branch Lines of Wiltshire* by Colin Maggs to understand the complications of the system.

CROFTON

The summit level of the canal is forty feet above this lock. To feed this top level, water has to be pumped from Wilton Water, an eight acre reservoir to the left of this photograph, into the Crofton Leat which runs west for a mile to Crofton Top Lock. Every time the lock is opened 70,000 gallons are lost and have to be replaced. Nowadays this water is pumped electrically but the original massive beam engines have been carefully restored to full working order by members of the Crofton Society. They are a popular attraction on 'steaming' days. Wilton Water is a result of damming the narrow valley above Wilton and is frequently teeming with interesting wildfowl.

CROFTON

The two Cornish beam engines are each capable of pumping up to 140,000 gallons an hour. The first was installed by Boulton and Watt in 1812 and the other by Harveys of Hale in 1845. It is thought that the former is the oldest steam engine in the world still in working order, in its original engine house, and doing the job it was built to do. The engines are 'in steam' on several weekends in the year and are certainly well worth a visit.

ST MARY'S CHURCH GREAT BEDWYN

A quiet stretch of the canal looking east towards Great Bedwyn and St Mary's Church. This fine church is built entirely of flint and dates from the 12th century with significant additions in the 15th. Among many interesting brasses and furnishings there is one particularly impressive Elizabethan monument to the memory of Sir John Seymour, whose daughter Jane married Henry VIII. The recumbent figure in full armour, sword at his side, lies on the tomb. The inscription on the wall above leaves one in no doubt of his dynastic significance and goes on to explain that he was first buried 'amongst divers of his ancestors, both Seymours and Sturmyes' in Easton Royal Priory but when that became ruined was reburied here in 1590. Outside the church there survives an almost complete preaching Cross.

FROG LANE GREAT BEDWYN

A row of thatched cottages across the railway and canal from the centre of the village. Great Bedwyn is now a quiet residential village but back in the Saxon era it was a market town of considerable importance. Its entry in the Domesday Book of 1086 makes interesting reading. 'The King holds Bedewinde. King Edward held it. It was never assessed or tithed. This town provides one night's entertainment for the King's household with all usual customs.' One would like to know more about the 'usual customs' for apparently the cost was around £100, considerably more than the rival settlements of Ramsbury and Aldbourne had to pay in geld tax. Bedwyn also had a Royal mint but this was later removed to Marlborough.

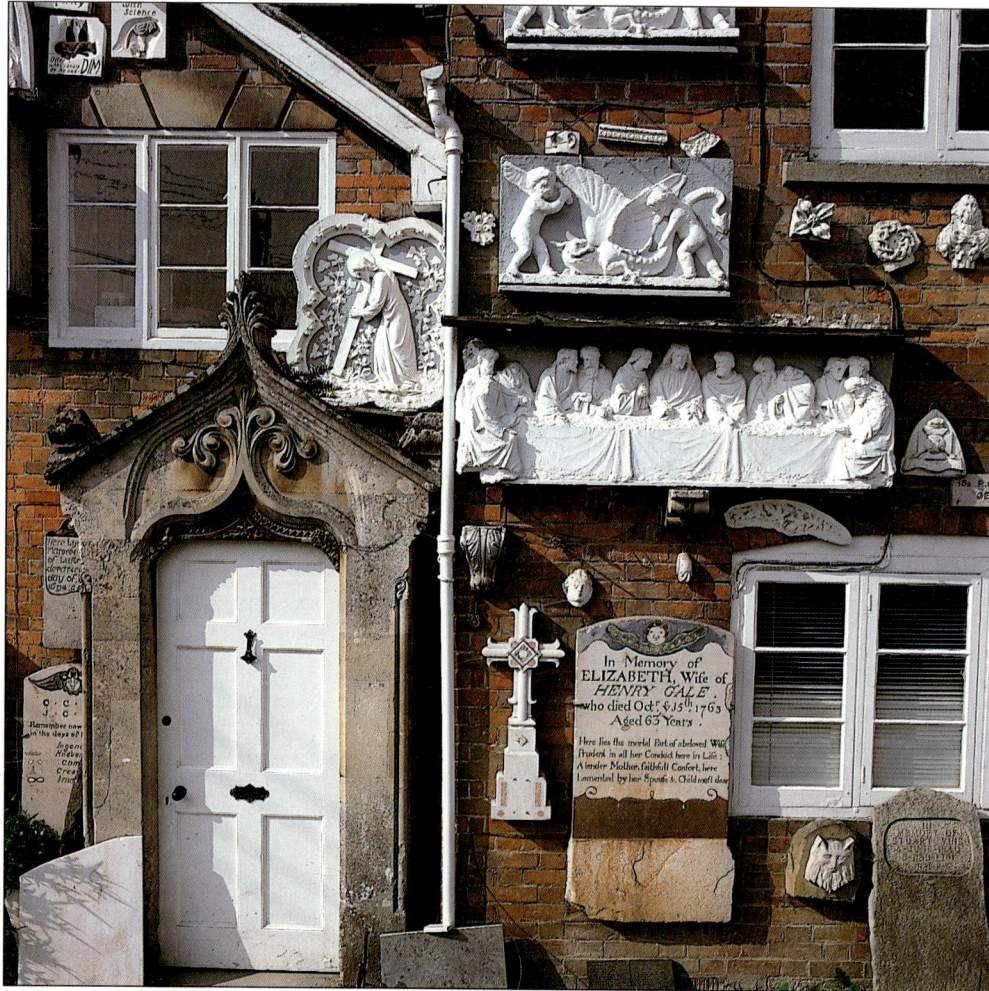

LLOYDS
GREAT BEDWYN

Just as Aldbourne was famous
for the church bells produced
by the Wells family foundry so
Bedwyn is renowned for the
Lloyd family tradition of stone
carving. Benjamin Lloyd
settled in Bedwyn after
working on the Bruce tunnel
during the construction of the
Kennet and Avon canal in 1803.
Seven generations later the
Lloyd workshops are still in
business and examples of their
work can be found throughout
the south of England. The
museum is a truly amazing
place displaying not only
statues, gravestones and
memorials - some with
amusing inscriptions - but also
the tools of the craft, old and
new. Visitors to the museum
are welcome to watch the
stonemasons at work.

GREAT BEDWYN

In modern democratic Britain
we are used to constant
changes in parliamentary and
local government boundaries,
but it took more than 600 years
for Bedwyn to lose the right to
elect two members to
Parliament. By the time of the
Reform Bill in 1832 Great
Bedwyn was considered a
'rotten' borough and paid the
price!

LITTLE BEDWYN

A row of Victorian houses on the west side of the canal and railway leading towards the Norman church of St Michael, whose fine stone spire is visible in the facing photograph.

MANOR FARM
LITTLE BEDWYN

This farmhouse stands right in the middle of the village with its attractive range of farm buildings across the road including this octagonal game larder surmounted by a weathervane in the shape of a hog's head. To the right of the house, not in this photograph, there is an interesting summerhouse, open on two sides, revealing the original 18th century plasterwork.

TIDCOMBE

A small hamlet facing north below Tidcombe Down around which the Roman road from Mildenhall to Winchester curves and climbs on to Chute Causeway to avoid plunging into the deep valley of Hippenscombe. The views from here are some of the most spectacular in Wiltshire - unspoilt by modern man, but pleasantly littered with old barrows, tumuli and earthworks left behind by his ancestors.

EAST GRAFTON

Looking across the Green towards the church of St Nicholas which was built in 1844 in the Norman style by Benjamin Ferrey. An interesting feature is the pyramid roof from which project carved symbols of the Evangelists and slightly above them the heads of four dogs. A sad accident happened during the building of the church. Its principal benefactor Lord Bruce took a friend to inspect the new roof only to see it collapse and kill him.

ALL SAINTS CHURCH FROXFIELD

Froxfield has the misfortune to be bisected by the busy A4 but it is nonetheless a pretty village with a well-tended Green and a number of interesting houses and cottages. In the churchyard there is an unnamed 1730 memorial simply stating 'Behold the World is full of Crooked Streets. Death is the Market Place where all Men Meets. If Life was Merchandize that Men could buy, The Rich would always Live the poor must Dye.' One wonders what motivated this outburst.

SOMERSET HOSPITAL FROXFIELD

A familiar landmark, but how many motorists hurtling through Froxfield know the story and purpose of this elegant building? In 1686 the Duchess of Somerset made provision in her will for an almshouse initially for thirty poor widows, and when the income from her endowment permitted for a further twenty. The section to the east of the entrance was built by 1694 and the rectangle completed in 1771 with the gatehouse and gothick chapel added by 1813. Today there continues to be accommodation for forty-nine women in self-contained flats or houses all of which have recently been modernised.

GREAT HALL
LITTLECOTE HOUSE

This must be one of the best collections of Civil War armour, buff-coats and firearms to be found in any private house. The Pophams supported Cromwell and this was the armour they provided for the troops they commanded. It is still arranged on the walls much as it was by Colonel Leybourne-Popham in the early l9th century. Down the middle of the hall which is beautifully lit by the floor to ceiling windows is the long shuffle-board table and beyond it a portrait of Sir John Popham.

CROMWELL CHAPEL
LITTLECOTE HOUSE

Being in the oldest part of the house this may well have started life as a pre-Reformation chapel but there is no doubting the Puritan spirit behind this design. There is a fine balustraded gallery on three sides but little sign of any carved or painted decoration and a rather severe raised pulpit where one might have expected to see an altar.

PRESTON TOLL HOUSE

Prior to the introduction of Turnpike Trusts in the early 18th century responsibility for roads lay with local parishes. Trusts were more efficient but were unpopular with the stagecoach trade, merchants and drovers who resented paying for what was formerly free. The tollgates were placed at strategic points where travellers could not avoid them. This one was presumably intended to gather tolls from travellers going to and from Aldbourne, Ramsbury and Hungerford. Certain categories of travellers such as pedestrians, church-goers on Sunday, the Royal Mail and people living locally did not have to pay and consequently tollgates were seldom built within a mile of towns or villages. The coming of the railway destroyed the Trusts whose income fell so sharply they were abolished within twenty years. Once again the roads became the responsibility of the rate-payers.

CHILTON FOLIAT

An attractive village with several very large Georgian houses, a good church and brick-built thatched houses like this one. On the edge of the village on higher ground above the road to Leverton is Chilton Lodge whose walled kitchen gardens were made famous in the recent television series on Victorian gardening. Much of the success of these programmes was due to the performance of the knowledgeable and engaging Mr Harry Dodson, head gardener here for over twenty years.

COBBLER'S LOCK HUNGERFORD

Here the river Dun passes beneath the canal under a three-arched aqueduct into Freeman's Marsh. Commoners Rights over this marsh and Port Common on the other side of the town were granted by John of Gaunt to the inhabitants of Hungerford. Over the years these rights to shoot, fish and keep cows on the Common have been steadfastly defended and are annually confirmed at the meeting of the ancient Hocktide Court on the second Tuesday after Easter. This is a day of considerable conviviality and the most celebrated in the Hungerford calendar!

ST LAWRENCE'S CHURCH HUNGERFORD

The old Norman church was becoming decrepit by the end of the 18th century and partially collapsed in 1814 following a heavy snowfall. It was demolished and because the canal had just been completed the new church was built of Bath stone. This must have been the site of the original settlement of Hungerford but for some reason, perhaps because it was too marshy the town was moved further to the east in the 12th century and laid out on either side of the present High Street.

HUNGERFORD WHARF

What is now an attractive landscaped open space overlooking the canal was once a busy commercial wharf and builders yard. It started life in 1798 when the eastern section of the canal to Reading was opened. Following its completion in 1812 more than 200 barges used the canal taking three days to travel from Newbury to Bath. The arrival of the railway very quickly killed off this long-distance trade. The wharf continued to be used for local business until closure in 1962. The redevelopment of the whole area has been skilfully handled and is a great asset to the town.

BRIDGE GARDENS HUNGERFORD

The thick foliage partially screens the very handsome iron footbridge leading from the first floor of the house to the street. This private bridge became necessary because when the canal, which passes close to the north of the house, was cut through the town the bridge over it raised the street way above the original front door.

TOWN HALL HUNGERFORD

Unlike so many towns in the south of England, Hungerford and Marlborough have somehow managed to protect their High Streets from the worst excesses of the retail boom of the 70's and 80's. This is not to say there has been no new building - far from it - but most of it has been carefully thought out and is not out of scale. This is a good example of a small development just off the High Street. The clocktower visible here is part of the Town Hall of which there have been four in the history of Hungerford. The first was declared 'ruinous and utterly dekayed' as far back as 1543 and was replaced in 1607 and again in 1786. These first three stood in the Market Place in the middle of what is now the High Street opposite Park Street. The present Town Hall which was also the Corn Exchange was completed in 1870.

BELOW STAIRS HUNGERFORD

Hungerford is rightly renowned for its antique shops. There is something here for every taste and pocket from the largest oak dresser to the smallest item of jewellery in the 'Arcade'.

DENFORD MILL

Old photographs show that this five-bay fulling mill was still working in 1904. The miller's house was at the right hand end - partly hidden behind the tree. Nearby Dunford Mill on another branch of the Kennet had the added benefit of being immediately adjacent to the canal and able to use it to transport goods to and from the side of the mill. It is noticeable that along the entire length of the canal, wherever it passed close to existing mills, considerable efforts had to be made to ensure that their water supply was not affected. The millers' rights were protected under the Kennet and Avon Canal Act.

KENNET AND AVON CANAL KINTBURY

Much the best way of seeing the canal and its countryside is to walk the towpath, but if that is not possible take a trip from Kintbury on this horse-drawn barge. A close inspection of the hillside to the right of this photograph, taken from Shepherd's Bridge, would reveal the ruins of several Whiting mills which once processed the local chalk into a fine powder used by the paint industry. It was despatched by barge to Bristol.

HAM HILL

The village of Ham lies between Shalbourne and Inkpen below this prominent line of hills. This has always been good farming land and records show that there has been a settlement here since before Domesday. Like many other villages relying on agriculture for employment, its population has steadily declined from a peak in the 18th century. But it has kept its identity and remains a small thriving rural community largely unaffected by 20th century development.

VILLAGE GREEN
HAM

Away from the Green with its attractive medley of thatched cottages, brick and flint houses and pub, lies the Manor and the church of All Saints. It has no particular architectural significance, although Pevsner does mention it, but it is nonetheless a real gem of a village church. Unlike many other churches, spoilt by over enthusiastic restoration work in the l9th century, All Saints had the good fortune to be 'modernised' in the 18th. The churchyard is dominated by a great yew, 18 feet in circumference, and there is a splendid collection of Georgian tombs and monuments. All is explained in a well written four page history available in the church.

COMBE GIBBET
INKPEN

The first gibbet was erected here in 1676 to display the bodies of George Broomham and his mistress Dorothy Newman hanged for the murder of his wife. As each succeeding gibbet has rotted away or been vandalised yet another has been erected - the fifth in 1992 apparently to cheers of applause followed by a barbeque. There is a story, perhaps apocryphal, that when this latest gibbet was raised someone climbed to the top to obtain a 'victim's-eye-view' but unaccountably made no effort to discover how the victims felt at the time! The view to the north across Inkpen to Kintbury and beyond is sufficiently spectacular from the ground for most people.

COMBE VILLAGE

The Iron Age hillfort on top of Walbury Hill just to the east of the gibbet, marks the highest point in Berkshire, higher even than Milk Hill overlooking the Pewsey Vale. The country south of here contrasts sharply with the lush Kennet valley to the north. It is a colder, thinner and more open country with fewer trees and less people. In the middle distance lies the village of Combe and to the right Combe Manor, beside which is the charming little church of St Swithun.

WARREN COTTAGES
VERNHAM DEAN

These cottages are on the southern slope of the hill overlooking the eastern end of the Hippenscombe valley. Such is its depth and angle of descent even the Romans admitted defeat and built their road around the edge of what is now called the Chute Causeway. There is however a track that leads in an almost straight line from Oxenwood, behind Fosbury House, down and across Hippenscombe Bottom and up and over the Causeway to Chute Standen. It is a four mile walk and the views are superb - a less arduous way of seeing much the same countryside is to drive along the Causeway from Oxenwood to Vernham Dean and back past Fosbury.

OXENWOOD

A tiny village whose name has become well-known throughout the county since its old school was converted into a Field Studies Centre. The wide range of courses organised from here for children of all ages has proved very popular with local schools.

THE HATCHET
LOWER CHUTE

The four villages that bear the name Chute all lie to the south of the Causeway in what remains of Chute Forest. Lower Chute has this lovely old pub and just around the corner a pretty village green. Upper Chute also has a pub and the only working church in the area. Chute Standen has the 18th century brick Standen House with its impressive facade. Chute Forest has Chute Lodge, a substantial brick house of the 18th century which has survived a period of being used as a Borstal and has now been restored. Here also is St Mary's Church with its tall shingle spire appearing above the trees. Unfortunately this fine Pearson church is no longer used and is in the care of the Redundant Churches Trust.

BIDDESDEN HOUSE

Before returning to Marlborough, attention must be drawn to one of the finest early 18th century houses in Wiltshire, if not in England. Biddesden House stands at the end of a long drive off the Chute road to Ludgershall. The house was built in 1711 by General Webb. It is of brick chequered in red and blue and the front part is seven bays square. Above the main entrance there are three distinctive round windows. On the east side there is a substantial castellated round turret said to have been designed to house a bell acquired in France by the general.

Over the years many distinguished authors and poets have found in Marlborough and its surrounding country a rich source of inspiration. Sir William Colt Hoare in the l9th century and William Stukeley in the 18th were the first to methodically research and record the antiquities of prehistoric Wiltshire. Since then there has been a huge output of published work on the archaeological history of the county, and Avebury, in particular, has been the subject of many books. The Civil War, the Kennet and Avon canal, and the development of the Railways have had their historians. Richard Jefferies, Alfred Williams, Charles Sorley, John Betjeman and Geoffrey Grigson are just a few of the many authors who have written about Marlborough.

Thanks to the enthusiastic support of two publishers, Ex Libris of Bradford on Avon and Countryside Books of Newbury, there is no shortage of books on local history or guide books for those wishing to walk the many footpaths in the area. The following short list is no way comprehensive but can be recommended with confidence and has the merit that the books are currently available. Anyone wishing to delve into local history in more detail will find the Wiltshire Library and Museum Service most helpful. Their headquarters is in Trowbridge.

A History of Marlborough J.E. Chandler White Horse Bookshop

The Marlborough Downs Kenneth Watts Ex Libris Press

Footprints Through Avebury Michael Pitts

A History of the Savernake Forest Marquess of Ailesbury

The Kennet and Avon Canal Niall Allsop

The Vale of Pewsey John Chandler Ex Libris Press

The Heart of a Village Ida Gandy Alan Sutton

The Village in the Valley Barbara Croucher

Touring Guide to Wiltshire Villages Margaret Wilson Ex Libris Press

The Wiltshire Village Book Michael Marshman Countryside Books

Wiltshire Churches Derek Parker, John Chandler Alan Sutton

Wiltshire, Buildings of England Nikolaus Pevsner Penguin

The Victoria History of Wiltshire Oxford University Press

Churches